# *AT THE* EDGE *OF* FOREVER

POEMS BY ANGEL ELISA COLLIER

BLUE LIGHT PRESS ◆ 1ST WORLD PUBLISHING

1st WORLD
PUBLISHING

SAN FRANCISCO ◆ FAIRFIELD ◆ DELHI

# At the Edge of Forever

Copyright ©2020 by Angel Elisa Collier

1st World Library
PO Box 2211
Fairfield, IA 52556
www.1stworldpublishing.com

Blue Light Press
www.bluelightpress.com
Email: bluelightpress@aol.com

Book & Cover Design
Melanie Gendron
www.melaniegendron.com

Cover & Illustration Concepts
Angel Elisa Collier

Cover Art
"Dog Woods" by Melanie Gendron

Interior Illustrations
Melanie Gendron

First Edition

Library of Congress Control Number: 2019956402

ISBN: 978-1-4218-3646-1

# ACKNOWLEDGEMENTS

Much appreciation to Diane Frank for her continued instruction, guidance and inspiration. A heartfelt thank you to JoLynn Gates and everyone involved in the creation of this book.

This book is my prayer for the trees,
polar bear, honeybee, pika, our precious songbirds,
the Indigenous People of North America
and for our beautiful Earth home,
shimmering like a jewel in space.


Please plant a tree, feed the birds, recycle,
drive less, use alternative energy,
or volunteer a little of your time
for an environmental cause.

i thank You God for most this amazing day:
for leaping greenly spirits of trees
and a blue true dream of sky;
and for everything
which is nature which is infinite which is yes.

— e. e. cummings

# CONTENTS

## AN APPALACHIAN FAMILY

## MOON OF FALLING LEAVES

## ASCENSION

# Morning Canticle

A robin dreams
inside the hidden light of trees.
Flute wind ruffles leaves
as melting sky
sheds its smoky feathers.

The sun opens its beaded purse,
spilling gold coins
into the woods.

Squirrel leaps
out of lemon pools of sunlight
in a scatter dance,
somersaults with a strip of bark,
tickling the soft belly of joy.

As I stand in a circle of budding trees,
wild birds string a jeweled necklace of songs.

This moment lingers
like baubles of rain
reflecting sky.

A hunger for wild things,
my body seeks to fold itself
into jay-blue wings,
balancing on the highest bough.
Clouds trundle across
the lapis wheel of cold sky.
When my throat swells
with the sweet elderberry of song,
I know one day
*I will fly.*

# Breath Of Aspen Trees

*After reading Sleeping in The Forest by Mary Oliver*

Each morning is born
wet, pink,
filled with light,
like the infant on Christmas.
My heart is opening,
an unfledged bird waiting
to catch the music of the moment.
Morning light scatters silk pods
through the trees.
Aspen trees rustling their golden robes,
apostles of peace writing scripture
across the blue scroll of heavenly sky.
I feel myself being touched
by the unseen.

Halfway to St. Gabriel,
they are the eyes of birds
whose sunlit wings follow
the sapphire curve of Earth,
stored inside the delicate, hollow bones
of memory.
A tiny flash of light
flies between my shoulders.

My heart aches
for the gentle eyes of a purple finch
already studying me,
little head leaning toward sunrise.
O what holiness
in this heaven of Earth!

The scent of pine resin
glues me to this place.
Nothing between me and the white fire
of cumulus clouds
but the multi-colored leaves of my thoughts,
floating like kites,
caught in the arms of trees.
Tiny eyes hide
beneath the tangled hair of field grass,
milkweeds, and remaining wildflowers
following the sun.

Dangling between heaven and necessity.
As I fall away,
do the trees tremble?
I close my eyes,
cleansing my spirit
with the holy water of peace,
heart dappled with leaf-song.
A psalm shivers on the brisk wind,
offering its voice to God.

## Autumn Refuge

When a bad day tightens its fist,
lift my breath to the ear of Mary Immaculate.

I surrender myself
on the grassy shore of dappled sky,
clouds floating over my shoulders
like guardian angels.
My body opens like a window.
This moment fills me
with soft veils of alabaster light.
The heavy wool of sky
sinks
down
to warm the naked trees.

Ethereal voices from the woods,
brown leaves shiver with messages
from the other world.
Furrowed bones creak in the stillness.
They sway with memories
like sweet rain holding wild birds —
the flutter of a thousand rapid heartbeats
in their arms, or apple perfume.

I stretch this moment
like long shadows
at the end of something.
An owl feathers the skeletal silence
with soft questions.
A nuthatch freckles the quiet
with gentle staccatos,
looking at the world

from a different angle.
Beneath the violet nocturne
of evening sky,
a downy woodpecker
flies into the dream of an oak tree.

As I walk that holy compass
called Earth,
nature remains my True North,
guiding my feet
across the alchemy of God.

# Feathers Of Light

The sky opens its cerulean window,
sun lifting over the trees
beaming through misty curtains.
I fill my hands
with the yellow bulbs of maple leaves.
Oak trees toss their copper coins
on bristled swatches of east wind.

As a rabbit turns white in the north,
crimson leaves fall
from my heart's corolla
into the deep water of happiness.
Autumn's quilt
sewn with marigold petals,
smoked leaves, migrating wings.

The pampas grass shivers.
Their silk filaments
dapple with seed pearls,
the color of creamed wheat.
They seem to glow from within.
Their soft breaths
feather my soul with God's tongue.

# Meditation In A Minor

From the eclipsed window of sleeping sky,
powdered milk wings of a moth
flutter over the lamp of Pleiades,
silver hieroglyphs etched into the cave.
A great horned owl
feathers my dreams with a velvet soliloquy.
Clusters of trees, like Buddhist temples.
Below them, little monks in armored robes
chanting.
As my soul merges into black leaves,
you trill in A minor,
before watching the sunrise
from the white slipper of a morning glory.

# White Flames Flickering In The Night Trees

Soft fur of night coils the neighborhood
like the plush roll of a black cat's dream.
Only a tree frog's buttery snore
and cricket in the fallow field,
sprinkle the quiet.
An owl wraps silent wings
around my soul,
under the white pearl of full moon.
Sky falls into the trees.
Fireflies flash in the leaves
like Christmas lights,
a hallelujah in the velvet shadow
of the Creator.

Through the misty shower of green light,
a falling star arrows
into the heart of a marigold,
flashing with every pulse.

## As Only Birds Know

Below the drowsy autumn sky,
vermilion leaves of light
scatter at my feet.
As the sun leaves this world,
stones bleed.
The petaled thumbs of wild aster
turn inward for light.

The sharp edges of my day soften.
Pain finds no home for its thorn
in a heart feathered with cardinals.

Wispy moon rises like smoke,
sifting through fading blue sands of sky.
From the green tassels of pine trees,
wren and robin
fold soft corners of evening
into the final aria.

Through an invisible portal,
a flutter of wings into a secret world.
As birds fly out of my eyes,
why is the sky so lonely?

# Ode To Pluto

Library shelves warp under Jupiter's gravity,
but you dodge the Hubble eye
with three billion miles
of intergalactic dust.
While others spin their heads
in the same direction,
you tilt 17 degrees
to the compass of your own hydrogen wheels.

Stripped of your identity,
evicted from the neighborhood,
an ice thimble rolls in solar dust,
tossed by the winds of Neptune.
Your walk around the block
takes 248 years.

Under eternal night,
the world is my skating rink.
Breathing through an oxygen space suit,
I hear the music of falling stars.

The blue air slaps my cheek with burning ice.
I build a nitrogen snowman
to keep my heart warm.

# Sparrow

*For my mother, Mary M. Gallay*

The woods fading paw prints
slowly dissolve into the silken pocket of shadows.
The sun's last flame flickers,
leaving only ashes.
All the birds have flown into silence.
The sky shatters.
Full moon untangles the snowy petals of its braids
through the pines.

She rests her head
inside the white wing of a goose.
As her small body turns gently on its axis,
she hears music through the shimmering
waterfall of moonlight.

Beneath the heavy eyelid of dreams,
a field sparrow pleats the sky
with ecru feathers.
They flutter around the soft echo of a memory,
a mottled egg
throbbing in the grass.
Quills stretch across the stars,
wings folding around her
with the rapid beating of a bird's heart.

# He Carries The Sky On His Wings

*For Daddy*

A plumed arrow flies through my house
with a heavenly cadence.
Melodies weave
between feathers of lavender light,
fluttering window curtains.
Millions of heart cells expand
as I hear you sing to me
from the throat-swell of a bluebird.
Perched on a shepherd's hook,
a bird house peg,
a vein between my shoulder blades.
Head leaning toward opening sky,
you look at me
blooming with every note:
*"I just want you to be happy.*
*Everything is alright."*

I grip the wild branch of this moment
with both feet
before the sky opens its blue wings,
lifting my heavy limbs
into the pink sprays of dawn.

# Two Jets

*For Frank and Mary Gallay*

To find you,
I must travel on my knees.
Soul reaching across the dimensions
for parents, long gone.
Violet petals of sky open
over bones of trees.

As a north-west wind releases my prayer,
the sun scatters its yellow leaves
around my feet.
My heart is a mirror
reflecting sky,
70,000 feet above the meadow
of my breathing.

On this Thanksgiving Day,
I am looking upward
to see you side-by-side through the blue,
flying.

# The Old Bird Woman

*Inspired by the song "Feed The Birds" by the Sherman Brothers*

Dawn's ruby fingers
lift the kite wings of wild birds,
the landscape chiseled with pine trees,
horse-drawn carriages and window boxes
painted with wild marigolds.
Pink puddles shimmer along street corners
from yesterday's rain.

She stumps toward the steps
of Saint Paul's cathedral
on fragile bird feet.
Crumbs scatter from her hand
like shooting stars.
Pigeons fly out of the white nest of her hair,
through the tattered window
of her burlap skirt,
into faded eyes.

The morning sky flutters
in a blur of violet, cyan and beige.
Pools of liquid love notes
gurgle from their slick, green throats.
She smiles at them
under drooping brows.

As sun-licked winds shake church bells,
doves float through the columns.
Saint Francis looks down from the gilded dome.
A white, misty light from the sky
funnels around the old woman.
Her spirit soars
to the top of a hickory tree,
singing.

# Blue Eyes In The Passing Train

*For Gene Tierney*

Slowly, I disappear
into feathers of a black and white dream,
a misty noir from 1945.

A shadow treads out of the fog,
blue eyes in the passing train,
silk robe draping over a Bergere chair.

She watches him from the living room, above the fireplace,
through swirls of gesso and cadmium blue.
A fedora of questions
boil inside an eggshell.

A sigh of Soir de Paris perfume
from moonlit petals
on the oriental rug,
violin winds from *Laura's Theme* by David Raksin
weave around a crystal vase
of white calla lilies.

Ivory walls echo rose-scented memories,
soft light refracts through champagne glass
as she recites Byron's "Pleasure in the Pathless Woods."
Smoke from a Turkish cigarette
curls around the verse,
pink petals of a rose opening
near a delicate overbite.

She unlocks her secrets
on lilac pages of trees.
But if you try looking over her shoulder,
she will melt into space.

# Polonaise For Chopin

### I.

Your first opus was a pair of lungs
bellowed from the Skarbek Villa in Zelazowa-Wola;
iron will in the language of your land.
That was February 22, 1810.
When your fame caught up with your shoe size,
you took a fistful of Poland in a silver box
and buried it in Paris.

Horse-drawn carriages echo in clinking burgundy glass,
as my mother recites your musical poem.
Your ivory dance are lilac petals on trembling water
flowing downstream. Pianoscapes of a child prodigy,
watercolor notes in the gallery of my living room.
I am happy under this tear.

### II.

Dreams sewn from nightingale wings
flutter across my ivory skin.
I tremble in your passionate hands
beneath the silver candle
drizzled with stars.
A lighthouse of fireflies
navigate through the nocturne.

### III.

Time melts
into liquid paraffin,
fading aroma
of canard a l'orange for two,
already cold.

Songbird lifts her wing
staring past the empty bench,
silent.
White feathers
reach for those fingers in Paris,
the Pere Lachaise graveyard,
heart buried at home in a Polish church.

Frederic, come back for an encore.

# Man From The Northwoods

*For Tom*

He takes a long walk
to the center of himself.
In his wrist I feel the pulse
of the forest, wrapping a verdant robe
around his shoulders
scented with balsam, wet leaves, musk.
The broken branch of his walking stick
supports him across fallen logs
and the barbed vines of his emotions.

Forcing his way through the brambles,
he follows the magnetic needle of his soul,
willow warbler dripping water pearls of song
from basswood leaves.
Thick moss clings to the memory
of where he walked,
a vertical void still murmuring.

Through fractals of time,
seeds collect around his ankles,
white violets bloom in his hand.
He composes a symphony
from shapes of sound:
the creaking spine of an old tree,
the cedar flute of a mourning dove,
chittering squirrel.
The forest's slow breath
wafts from his lungs,
but the aspen tree
remains speechless.

# Winds Of Silence

All night on the horizon
where the sun lies vigil,
silence sharpens its silver blade
across the ice fields.
I hear feathers falling.
My tongue freezes in this glacial church.
Even the murmur of my thoughts
fracture the stillness.
I sculpt this moment
from blocks of ice,
petrel wings, black eyes crying.
The white wind swallows my breath.
The stark beauty
of this holy other-world
fill my eyes with salt.

Floating ships of blue glass
carry my eyes
across an island of Weddell seals.
The sun hangs like a pearled brooch
inside a copper halo,
pulling rainbows out of refracting crystals.
Chalky cliffs thunder into the icy sea.
Great white pyramids chiseled by wind,
glow turquoise under the surface,
grinding across the ice floes.

A thousand masks of blue
surround me
cooling earth's fire,
a refuge from all things human.

The wind howls like wolves
across the deep, white space.
Green flames flicker over the mountains
shooting sparks into constellations.
I retreat into the warm tent of my soul
to remember who I am.

# In Praise Of The Great White Bear

Evening sky bleeds into the clouds,
stretching from a world beyond the curve.
As the day collapses into itself,
soft shadows climbing
through my window,
I fold into silence.

Winds off Svalbard
slap my cheek with a white paw,
claws rip through wool
reaching bone.

White mountains bending sky,
charred with swirling violet fire.
Arctic fox scampers into my dream
inside blue glass,
tilting on its axis.
Behind the hazel eyes of sleep,
the polar bear's shoulder
carries me across the fjords,
paddling the shadows.

Heavy feet
plod the immaculate shore.
Belly muscles twitch through fur,
every hair a filament of light.
A grunt,
slow, weighted breath,
her nose poking the air for a meal.
Across the fallow ice fields,
I watch patience
sitting silent by the breathing holes.

All the stars begin to thaw.
The sun, like a small white bird,
slowly flies across the horizon.
I awaken,
fragments of a dream shimmering
under feathered sunlight
and in the opening eyes of a polar bear.

# Nowhere Else To Go

*This poem calls attention to global warming, while still being hopeful for positive change. Although the pika could conceivably replace the panda as the next icon for species preservation, there are examples showing improvement, like the Northwestern United States.*

The moon's steady stare
glows from indigo sky
that carries the new day in its womb.
Tiny paws of light across the Rockies
release the ghosts of wildflowers.
Jagged peaks wade in the afterbirth.

As morning sky opens its jay-blue wings,
a warbler's honeyed breath
wafts from the east.
Music to make the trees shiver.

A high-pitched bleat
tickles the soft belly of my spirit.
Where colors shimmer from tumbling boulder fields
baptized with snow,
a pika carries the mountain
in her bones.

Waterfalls of sunlight
splash over the mountain farmer
bailing hay.
Wild iris, fireweed, purpleweed
bloom in the cracks.

As the mountain weeps,
she climbs a little higher,
the Earth's blue eye
glazed with fever.

Will she melt with the snow,
or follow the breath clouds
of a northwest wind
for the cool salve of an ice field?

# Flight Of The Monarch

I.

Flames break from the horizon,
igniting the meadow.
A watercolor of zinnias
open beneath stained-glass

II.

I am swallowed
by the crisp, white linen sky,
rattling the silence
with my teeth.
Jagged rocks rise beneath my feet
as I walk along the shore,
remembering to breathe
between thirty foot icy waves.

The clouds open a seam.
A wafer of sunlight
flutters across my left shoulder.
Heaven on earth
is found in the eternity of now.

III.

On the soft thumbs of yellow coneflowers,
sipping crystal bowls of dew.
Into the northwest wind,
a weightless surrender.
The empty air still dancing
with the memory of wings.

IV.

I'm scattering milkweed seeds
across the field.
They float into sky like votive candles
lit with sunlight,
a prayer
already answered.


V.

Hope stirs between silk threads,
unfurling its damp, crumpled wings
out of a dream.
They lean against the sun,
lifting into blue choir loft of sky,
church windows
reflecting light.

*AN APPALACHIAN FAMILY*

# John-Boy's Window

I.

As sleep flows like warm milk
over Walton's Mountain,
the nightingale weaves tendrils of a lullaby
into silk dreams.
Cricket strums a mountain dulcimer
as a falling star
lands in Mary Ellen's catcher's mitt.
Shadows dilate,
wild eyes grope the familiar.

Reaching into the sable pocket
of a deer's eye,
a solitary light burns
in the upstairs window.
From a slat writing desk, liquid thoughts
spill out of an ink bottle,
silent chatter
across the pages of a Big Chief tablet.

II.

The earth rises up
with its crooked spine,
kissing the flushed cheek of sky.
Misty blue waves rippled with pine,
wildflowers and serrated rock,
cool the prickly skin of mid-summer.

A white-tailed deer
leaps out of the nib of a fountain pen
beneath the white pine.

Pink trilliums bloom out of his hand
onto the empty page,
where winds sweep down from the mountain
carrying a bouquet of honeysuckle,
and the valley burns
with tiny bulbs of forget-me-nots.

As birds morph into trees,
John-Boy folds the silk edges of early evening
into the final chapter.

# A Walk Through Time

Grandpa, you are morning sky
holding birds in your hands,
igniting the old trails
as we walk through vanilla,
ponderosa pine and sunlit dreams.

When I touch the crinkled bark
of Grandma's hand,
I feel the roots
of all our ancestors.

## On Strike

Mama rides out of the kitchen
on her new bicycle,
laughter beaded with lark and blue jay,
scented with pine.
Swatches of brisk wind
ventilate her spirit
in the Baptist church choir.

## The Musician

Jason follows the compass of his fingers,
raindrops freckle the honeyed trail
of an old, upright piano.
Wild roses bloom in the treble clef.

## The Aviator

As time deepens his voice,
the sky falls into his eyes.
He sputters across frosted blue glass
and carries the morning sun
on silver wings.

# A Tree Cries In The Backyard

As death sheds its black petals
in Elizabeth's heart,
an oak treehouse
lifts her four year old feet
into lavender balm of sky.
Misty clouds lick the air,
saturated with the memory
of a gentle purr.

# MOON OF FALLING LEAVES

# Vision Quest

Silver trees drink from lactating moon.
River of stars
flood Kicking Bird with lullabies.
Pearled leaves shiver under his breath
rippling in moonlight.
Sweetgrass, buffalo bone marrow,
dried cottonwood leaves and tobacco
waft smoke signals through a clay pipe
into the stars.
Owls are silent sentinels
guarding the wild prairie of his heart.
His fingers reach across the fireflies,
but touch nothing.

Memories from the womb
are calling him back,
poles of willow lashed together under a dome of bear skins.
Seven stones hiss and glow,
sweat cascading over the mountain cliffs
of his shoulders.
Out of a high pitched wail,
an ancient Lakota song
drums against the soft hide of darkness.
Inside the wool of steam and burning sage,
he surrenders.

# Across The Bones Of His Ancestors

Along the scattered teepees,
cottonwood trees expose abandoned nests.
The last leaf dangles its life on a branch.
Lacework of ice crystals cling against cold stone.
Prairie rose sunrise blooms
in the feathered sky.
Kicking Bird flicks tobacco into the wind.
His cold shadow on the fading grass
saunters across the bones of his ancestors.

Crossing his arms,
his body guides the creek-brown horse.
Hooves pockmark the earth,
carrying the burdens of his master.

Golden-pink light leans against Kicking Bird
in a weightless embrace.
While humpback bearded chiefs
pound smoke from hooves on fire,
he can hear their breath rustle through the reeds.
Floating in watery gold,
his long, brown fingers
graze across the tall prairie grass.
Full lips pursed, as he nods in thought.
Eyes scan the landscape.

Through forty moons of falling leaves,
wisdom sculpts deep rivers
in the vaulted ceiling of his copper brow.
The mahogany earth of his eyes
from where everything grows,
linger on the horizon.

From beaded deerskin moccasins,
the wild totem of a holy man
climbs the sky.
Eagle feathers fan his head,
autumn skin stretches over thousand-year heirlooms,
black river hair
spills heavily down his back.
Buffalo tassels dangle from embroidered hide
on broad, heavy shoulders
that defy winter winds. . .
you can almost hear his breath
rustle through the reeds.

Fringed buckskin
follows the shape of muscled thighs
around the barrel of his horse.
A deep, guttural grunt, a stern face
turns toward the wild stretch of loneliness.
He wears thoughts like a buffalo robe,
translating messages from the Spirit World.

# Falling

A meadowlark's yellow song
opens the marbled sky.
Cumulus clouds sundance
across the turquoise sky in her eyes.
Kicking Bird follows his old, internal compass
as the Earth turns them
toward each other.

At the edge of cottonwood trees,
owl feathers quiver in the wind
over the beaded hide of her shoulders.
Black leaves of her braids
tumble past wide cheekbones.
Chiseled into the landscape
among ruffled collars of white water lilies.
Small lines etch
around the deep earth of her eyes.
The soft scar between her shoulder blades
betrays a deeper truth than beauty.

Beneath the steepled rock,
his hand paddles the red river
along her thigh.
The edge of a healing circle
ripples with sage.
He pulls the drawstring made of sinew,
as the soft mouth of a deer
opens in silent expectation:
sweetgrass, bear root,
red willow bark, cattail pollen,
turtleshell rattle.
Spotted eagle wings flutter around the circle
in a yuwipi healing song.

As the north wind grows teeth,
Kicking Bird leans into its thrust,
warming his fingers over the open wound.

## Surrendering To Gravity

Beneath the fire of setting sun,
a distant wolf laments
on top of a rocky cliff.
Time weaves Indian blankets,
as their hands scatter air molecules
to find each other.
Autumn snow pressing into soft, red earth.

Above the voices of trees,
an oasis of creamy fountains
inside a vault if deepening indigo.
Riding horseback across the prairie,
she feels Kicking Bird
lean heavily against her heart.
Snow geese point their compass south,
black tip wings wave good-bye
to another summer,
their white breasts
melt into western sky.

A message written in eagle quill
surrenders to gravity
through soft tissues of wind,
pirouettes and quietly settles
between their longing.

*ASCENSION*

# Letting Go

The sun retracts its red claws
as translucent vines splattered with stars
engrave the wild forest inside a bears' eye.
All the trees are on fire.
Half-eaten pears decompose
in the long, damp shadows.
Grass seeds scatter like dead ladybugs.
The night sky buttons its velvet cape
with a pearl brooch.

Memories torn by a northwest wind.
Rose perfume fades
from the petals of her shoulders.
The withered bell of her face
weeps into the bones of the forgotten.
Sepals of her faded dress
scatter over first snow.
The thorns she carried
turn to mulch.
Roots of gravity
rip from its labyrinth
by hands that once held her.

## The Edge Of Forever

Beyond sound,
cathedrals float among silver orchids
in violet shadows.
Cumulus towers heralding angels,
crystal wind shimmering its liturgy
like ripples of light on water.
Nebulous parthenons glow from within.
Burning prayer candles
ignite the edges of nimbus clouds.

Where gilded threads fray,
an ethereal window breaks open
to an explosion of sparkling white light.
Fountains of golden pink luminance
flare out to me,
refracting through my spirit.
Near the billowy arch
quilted with doves,
Christ's breath floats above my shoulders,
mouth full of soft rain
as I'm held in a baptism
of Divine Love.

# Under The Influence Of Angels

I float toward shining white light
at the end of a swirling blue tunnel.
Through the portal,
white blossoms snow into my eyes
from fragrant clouds of linden trees.
Petals of light
scatter across the forest path
where a gleaming white dog waits
under an archway of trees,
fur sparkling like musical notes
against violin strings of sunlight,
the ghostly shape of a wing
hovering over her left shoulder.

The forest opens
to a choir of perfumed color.
A hosanna of blue roses, pink gardenias
and white peonies
bloom into my eyes,
shimmering like kaleidoscopic mirrors
as they change hues,
blooming
and re-blooming
with every cadence.

Angels hover above my eyes,
wearing shimmering gowns
of glass and spun sugar,
all my Earthly prayers
clutched inside their wooden beads.

Aeolian chants
flow through legato strings.
Pearled voices
weave through a wild forest of birdsongs
praising God.
Iridescent wings of melody
lift me into the choir.
An altar of clouds fill with light.
My heart is as big as the sky.

# Beyond The Flight Of Birds

As I flutter out of my bones,
a sparkling river of cord
severs from my body.
I squeeze through a crack in the window,
to the radiant light outside.
The scent of balsam
waiting for birds,
lingers over my soul.
The voice that sang me to sleep
welcomes me home
from the feathered song of a cardinal.

As my spirit lifts high over the trees
above the waterfall of sky,
I release my breath,
scattering into a thousand pools of light,
kissing the feet of God.

## A Light In The Forest

I walk with my brother
through the deep secrets of trees
floating past my shoulders,
sweeping open amethyst petals of sky
across the spirit world.
Sunlight leaves luminous fingerprints
over black trees.
The air surges with sodden leaves,
resin, chamomile, oak moss.
He plucks a sprig of pine needles.
Lifting its sigh, he hears rain,
a flutter of wings,
a choir of angels.

I feel the warm glow of his arm
across my back.

# Paws Of Light

The sky opens with violet wings
like a morpho butterfly,
clouds floating through lavender.
Whiskers of grass shiver
in sun-swizzle and berry wind.
Eternal morning.

Wildflowers bloom in my eyes.
Tiny feet of white light
knead the silent place
across my heart.
Our cheeks rub together
throwing sparks.

We share a cup of catnip tea,
dreaming in a bed of birds and white carnations
as I watch you
holding the sun between your paws.

# I Hear The Cows Breathing

Bluebell sky
fills with the shimmering face of the Divine,
dropping pearls of light
on the tongues of tall grass,
bending colors through the mist.

Damselflies wrap blue ribbons
around the gift of now.
Monarch wings flutter out of the sun.
Wet paw-prints walk across creek stones
to sun-freckled cat dreams
beneath the white pine.
Buttercups ruffle their yellow aprons
in the open palm of the Creator.

Zen cows shimmer in honeyed pools of light
beaming through oak trees.
The scent of sweet churned grass
ferments in the cloud-flecked hours of eternity.
The gravity of their eyes
shine like fresh rain.
I suckle the warm milk of this moment,
hearing the ebb and flow of their breathing
as I walk deeper and deeper into pasture.

# To Walk With The Snow Leopard

After the last rose finch
flutters away remnants of summer wind,
bar-headed geese shatter the bleached silence
like wild, whooping warriors.

I walk with the snow leopard
over mountains of light
through swirling snow.
Footprints disappear
into another dimension.

# Resurrection

Out of an astral-blue lake,
mist opens its wings like swans,
lifting through the trees.
Songs of invisible birds
scatter feathers
into Heaven's hungry mouth.

The cool breath of evergreens
wreathed with pearls,
swell above the landscape of my solitude.
Flight dappled with gold
nest on the blue flame of sky.

The cloud sparkles with silver orbs
floating on a slow breeze of solo cello,
shaking the dew of piano notes
fluttering under its breath.
As I stand beside tall trees, it lingers
just on the other side of loneliness.
Over my shoulders, mist folding.
It glows rose pink
as I feel my parents embrace me
from the inside out.
Memories open like the sky:

a green canvas tent by the river,
daddy's reassuring voice,
mother's hand stroking my cheek.

Their thoughts have Hungarian accents.
Words falling like snow,
complete, silent,

as Alpine mountains reflecting light,
words that melt
as they touch my soul.

# Masterpiece

I slide off the paintbrush.
Fluted coral, yellow ochre, burnt sienna,
birthed on the other side of the Artist's thumb
in this Heavenly wilderness.
Beryl-blue petals of happiness
open to a crimson wash
across gessoed sky.
Metamorphosis under a sable brush,
flutter of monarch wings
on the green leaf of my shoulder.

A nectar of watercolor
showers from my tongue
beneath a helicopter of iridescent ruby.
I long to pour this moment
into a glass,
a honeyed flower of berries, fresh rain,
and evergreen.

My feet tunnel through deep silence.
They entwine with roots of wildflowers,
aquamarine grass
and the Guardian Angels of trees
that brush the soft edges of my body,
blending into the landscape.

# Tiger

A small fire burns
among the pleated skirts of bamboo.
Large paws leap across my heart
exposing a bullet hole
between the copper flames of a body
filled with light.

# Beneath The Primrose Sky

Sunlight lifts above the echo
of house wrens, splashing into the woods,
where rivers run together
between the trees
into an ocean of light.

Meadowlark beads a bracelet of song,
while crickets seed fields of warm grass
with their tropical bells.
I watch a bumblebee drink honeysuckle wine
from a petaled goblet.
Dandelions shake their fuzzy ghosts
into the next dimension.

This moment breathes
out of the lungs of pine trees,
fluttering my powdery wings
over buttercup and thistle.

A bunny sinks her damp paws
into the fertile earth of my happiness.
On the other side of touching,
a deer nibbles the embroidery of violets
stitched across the meadow's green apron,
no longer on the edge
of love and trembling.

# Spirit Of Trees

## I.

Somewhere near Lake Superior,
I held a pine tree in my arms.
I felt it sway
as its boughs breathed out forest.
Lichen drapes their bodies like icicles.
Violets bend where feet were searching.
As I lay on my back,
moss cushions the knife-edged stone I carry.
Prayers scatter their seeds
across this heaven.

## II.

Birch tree lifts my eyes
over smooth layers of parchment
curling around my fingers.
As they paddle its white river,
earthly perfume lifts above the green floor,
an echo of raindrops
between the branches.
Streamers of cardinal wind
rustle leaves around my shoulders.
Wearing wild birds in my hair,
I embrace the sun.

## III.

Through the pink whorl of a shell,
I hear the pulse of a redwood tree.
When I touch the serrated wound,
my fingers bleed.

My prayers
spiral into a southwest wind.
I tremble.
As conifer needles weep into the ground,
I feel skin break
the pages of my memory.
Metal teeth drill through my body,
spitting bark and bone
until I crack my spine on the forest floor.

White wings flutter upwards
out of the swish of fallen branches.

# Treehouse

*Inspired by the poem "Evening At Skane" by Rilke*

## I.

Divine light melts the stars,
releasing my spirit from its cage.
Held in the sky's cornflower-blue palm,
curlicues of song
swell from my tongue,
leaning into the same wind
the trees feel.

## II.

Through a curtain of oak leaves,
anticipation bakes
from a half-log trestle:
a bird's nest filled with French chocolate eggs,
Hungarian pastries served in apple blossoms,
a labyrinth of sugared, poppy seed noodles
fill a cedar bowl.

Beneath my fingers,
Debussy's Arabesque #1 flows
out from a piano carved from sculptured ash.
Silent pages of trees
wait for poetry.
White canvas leans against a wooden easel
looking at me with a blank stare.

## III.

I listen to pines breathing in the forest.
Oak trees rustle their green skirts,
pockets stuffed with acorns.
My house is filled

with the soft fists of sleeping birds,
the walls and ceilings flutter with dusky wings.
Hovering branches of leaves hang like a lampshade
over the luminous bulb of full moon.

I string each moment ...
muted whistle of cricket,
inquisitive owl,
tree moaning in the feathered arms
of east wind,
into a shimmering necklace of lullaby.
As I rock into the loamy textures of a dream,
I plant stars in the tall grass
and on petaled cheeks of morning glories.

# Ecstasy

Heaven opens its blue book of psalms
over a hallelujah of mountains.
Waterfalls shatter like frosted glass
into shimmering river.
Rainbows hover like ghosts
over the supernova.
As I surrender my soul into the roar,
how much ecstasy can I stand
without breaking?

# Mist Over Lake Superior

Slow waves rolling
out of the f-holes from a cello,
legato to the shore.
On violin strings,
high notes splash against my skin.
Under the moonlit sonata of silver sky,
he stands on a peninsula of jagged rock.
I am seized by his dark, moody gaze
beneath the black cloud of pompadour.
When the thunder of his eyes
storm across the violet skies of my own,
*"What took you so long?!"*
rains from his desperate kiss,
as our spirits rise
like mist over the rocky shore.

# Holy Communion

Where stained-glass angels sip wine
from a golden chalice,
beams of white light
explode from the heart of a carpenter
into the bones of my cathedral.

# About The Author

Angel Elisa Collier published her first book, *The Zen Of Falling Leaves*, in 2016. She follows up with her second book of poetry, *At The Edge Of Forever*. For several years, she has studied under the direction of poet and author Diane Frank. Angel is the recipient of the H. Edward Cannon Memorial Award for the poem "Polonaise For Chopin." She grew up among the woods and rolling hills of Minnesota and Wisconsin. She received her B.A. in Art at Maharishi University in Fairfield, Iowa, where she currently resides.

www.ingramcontent.com/pod-product-compliance
Lightning Source LLC
Chambersburg PA
CBHW032028090426
42741CB00006B/768